STEWARDSHIP
Program Builder
No. 1

Compiled by Paul M. Miller

It is suggested that three copies of this book be purchased, one for the director and two to cut apart for distribution to participants. Photocopying is prohibited.

Lillenas Publishing Company
Kansas City, MO 64141

Contents

Financial Stewardship 3

A Baseball Glove, by James Mulholland 3

An Obedient Steward, by Beverly Sargent Larsen 6

You'll Never Guess, by Elaine L. Schulte 8

Counting the Cost, by Kevin Stoltz 9

The Sacrifice of Love, by Barry Kolp 11

For Where Your Treasure Is, by Bette Dale Moore 27

Stewardship of God's Creation 36

The Conversion of Dastardly Dan, by Diana P. Ludwick 37

Sarah Mae's Offering, by Gail Blanton 41

Financial Stewardship

Scripture Arrangement for Responsive Reading

To those who through the righteousness of our God and Savior Jesus Christ have received a faith as precious as ours: What kind of people ought you to be?

You ought to live holy and godly lives. So then, dear friends, make every effort to be found spotless, blameless

And at peace with him.

Honor the Lord with your wealth, with the firstfruits of all your crops.

Then your barns will be filled to overflowing. "Bring the whole tithe into the storehouse, that there may be food in my house."

"Test me in this," says the Lord Almighty.

"And see if I will not throw open the floodgates of heaven."

"And pour out so much blessing that you will not have room enough for it."

2 Peter 1:1; 3:11, 14; Proverbs 3:9-10; Malachi 3:10

A Baseball Glove

by James Mulholland

Luke 6:38; Matthew 18:3

Cast:
FATHER
ANDY

Props:
Small paper sack
A baseball glove

(The front porch of a house. On the steps sits ANDY, *eight years old, looking into a paper sack. His father enters with a baseball glove in his hand.)*

FATHER: Want to play catch, Andy?

ANDY *(quickly hiding the sack):* Naw.

FATHER *(surprised):* No? What's wrong? Are you sick?

ANDY: No. I just don't feel like it.

FATHER *(sitting down next to* ANDY): Well, what do you feel like?

ANDY: I don't know.

(They sit in silence for a moment.)

ANDY *(nervously):* Dad, would you be really mad at me if I lost my baseball glove?

FATHER *(angrily):* What? You mean you lost your glove?

ANDY *(quickly):* No.

FATHER *(suspiciously):* They why did you ask me if I'd be mad?

ANDY: I just wondered.

FATHER: Andy, where is your baseball glove?

ANDY *(sighing):* I don't have it no more.

FATHER *(upset):* Come on, Andy. Stop playing games. Just admit it. You were careless and you lost your glove.

ANDY *(defensively):* I wasn't careless. I gave it to somebody.

FATHER *(disgusted):* What? You mean you loaned somebody that brand-new glove that cost us almost $20.00?

ANDY: I didn't loan it.

FATHER *(confused):* Well, what did you do then?

ANDY *(reluctantly):* Well, I sort of gave it away.

FATHER *(losing control):* Gave it away? To whom?

ANDY: Billy Johnson.

FATHER *(sternly):* Well, young man, tomorrow morning you're going to march right up to Billy Johnson and demand your glove back.

(ANDY *bows his head in obvious misery.)*

ANDY: Do I have to?

FATHER: Of course. You don't give your things away.

ANDY: Why not?

FATHER: Well, because . . . well, because you don't. I mean, Andy, why did you give it away? Did you trade it for something?

ANDY: Well, yeah.

FATHER *(disgusted):* I thought so. What?

(ANDY *pulls out the paper sack and hesitantly hands it to his father. His father opens and looks inside.)*

FATHER *(shocked):* Three marbles, some bottle caps, and a baseball card? This is what you traded for that glove?

ANDY *(defensively):* That's all he had to trade!

FATHER: And you just had to trade?

ANDY: No, but he liked my glove so much, and he didn't have one.

FATHER: Do you always give your things away to people who like them?

ANDY: No, just to Billy!

FATHER: What's so special about Billy?

ANDY: He's my best friend.

FATHER: Well, you tell your best friend to have his dad buy him his own glove.

ANDY: Billy doesn't have a dad, and his mom never has any money. He doesn't have any friends 'cause he wears real old clothes, and they're always dirty. I'm Billy's friend, and—

FATHER *(still angry):* So you felt sorry for him and gave him your glove.

ANDY: Yeah, 'cause in Sunday School they told us that Jesus said that if somebody asks for your coat, you're supposed to give it to them.

FATHER *(trapped):* Well, did Billy ask for your glove?

ANDY: No.

FATHER *(uncomfortable):* Well, then you shouldn't have given it to him.

ANDY *(about to cry):* I guess I just wanted Billy to be happy. I told him how happy I was 'cause you bought me my glove, and he said he wished that he had a dad to give him things. So I just thought having my glove might make him happy. I'm sorry, Dad. I'll make him give it back tomorrow.

(ANDY *bows his head while his father squirms uncomfortably with the sudden realization that his son doesn't deserve his anger.)*

FATHER *(putting his arm around* ANDY): No, Andy. You're right . . . I was wrong.

(ANDY *looks up in surprise.)*

FATHER: Jesus does want us to give to others. Even baseball gloves. I'm very proud of you. I'm glad I have a son who cares enough about his friend to give him an expensive baseball glove.

ANDY *(hopefully):* Then Billy can keep my glove?

FATHER *(laughing):* Yes. I tell you what. Why don't you see if Billy can come over tomorrow and play catch with us?

ANDY *(excited):* Really, Dad? That would be great.

FATHER: Of course, we'll just have two gloves.

ANDY: Well, you can hit 'em to us.

FATHER *(smiling):* All right.

ANDY *(sighing happily):* Boy, I can't wait to tell Billy that I get to share my dad with him.

(FATHER *and* ANDY *both smile.)*

An Obedient Steward

by Beverly Sargent Larsen

I am a steward of all I possess.
    My time.
    Everyone is given 24 hours.
    But it is *my* time!
        My time to caress.
        "Is it, My child?"
            (God is craving my attention.)
        "Are you sharing your time wisely
            with those in need?
        Are you wasting precious, fleeting moments
            on selfish ambitions?
        Are you studying My Holy Word?
            And talking to Me
                as often as I need to hear your voice?
        Are you a good steward of your time?"

I am a steward of all I possess.
My talent.
Not everyone is blessed with talent.
No need to concern myself.
I guess.

"Wait a minute, My child."
(God is turning my face—again.)
"Everyone has many talents. Musical. Oral.
All for service to others.
Use your abilities to glorify Me.
I gave them to you—
not to ignore,
but to seek out and fulfill.
'To whom much is given—much is required.'
Are you a good steward of your talents?"

I am a steward of all I possess.
My money.
Everyone has money.
I need all I have. Others can give.
I have less.

"My child, I gave you *all* you have."
(My eyes looked heavenward.)
"A tithe is all I ask.
Offerings will shower you with blessings.
Those who show wisdom in management
will reap earthly and heavenly rewards.
Give.
And serve Me!
Are you a good steward of your money?"
An obedient steward of all I possess.
My time.
My talents.
My money.
I am abundantly blessed!

My Father.
Use my hands, my feet.
Let them be swift for You.
Use my voice, my lips.
Let them be filled with words from You.
Use my silver, my gold.
Let them be powerful as You choose.
My moments and days are Yours.
My heart, my love is Yours.
Take me, use me, Lord.
I am Your steward—of all I possess.

You'll Never Guess

by Elaine L. Schulte

Cast:
MAN
WOMAN
YOUTH

(To be delivered in a lighthearted manner except for the serious appeal to the congregation at the end.)

MAN *(grinning at congregation):* You'll never guess what we're going to talk about the week before Stewardship Sunday [or whatever event your church is holding]. *(Turns to* WOMAN *and* YOUTH) What do you think?

WOMAN *(knowingly):* I have an idea that it's about making a commitment for the Lord's work here next year.

YOUTH *(with mock seriousness):* Something that's more than a tip on God's tablecloth.

MAN: More than a tip on God's tablecloth? Say, that's good!

YOUTH: I read an interesting quote about giving . . . that giving for God's work is the confession of our unpayable debt at Calvary.

MAN *(impressed):* That's true. I think that commitment means giving for God's work with a cheerful heart too.

WOMAN: That's from 2 Corinthians 9:7. "Each man should give what he has decided in his heart to give, not reluctantly or under compulsion, for God loves a cheerful giver."

MAN: It seems to me that we're bound in stewardship to take care of this earth until we get the better one.

WOMAN *(musing):* And that means *our* part of the earth too, right here in this community, right here in this church. You know, when you think about it, it's a joy and a privilege to help people around us. Our help goes much further when we give through the church, and people know that we give because we love the Lord.

YOUTH: W. H. Greever said that stewardship is what we do after we say, "I believe."

MAN *(thoughtfully):* That's an interesting way of putting it: "what we do after we say, 'I believe.'"

WOMAN: We've been giving a lot of money this year for so many things, but I know that we can't outgive God.

YOUTH: Elizabeth Barrett Browning said that God's gifts put man's best dreams to shame.

MAN *(does a double take at youth):* You read a lot of quotes, don't you?

YOUTH *(nods):* How about Winston Churchill: "We make a living by what we get, but a life by what we give." *(Pause)* And how about Billy Graham: "God has given us two hands—one for receiving and one for giving."

WOMAN: And how about Publius Mimus? *(If using scripts, does a double take at script)* Publius Mimus?? *(Seriously)* "He gives twice who gives quickly."

YOUTH *(with sudden sadness):* But what do I have to share?

WOMAN: Well . . . we have money, of course, but we have our time and talents to share too. And . . . apparently *you* have a lot of quotes!

YOUTH *(pleased):* I even have another one, this by John Wesley. "Make all you can, save all you can, give all you can."

MAN: I have one too, from 2 Corinthians 9:8 (Phillips). "God can give you more than you can ever need, so that you may always have sufficient for yourselves and enough left over to give to every good cause." *(Seriously to congregation)* Won't you joyously consider what you can give next year to do the Lord's work through this church?

Counting the Cost

Readers Theater

by Kevin Stoltz

Cast:

READER 1
READER 2
READER 3

R1: What He has said is most difficult.

R2: Yes, for what He has demanded from us

R3: is our all.

R1: He asked me of my family.

R2: Of me He asked of my estate.

R3: And from me, my kingdom.

R1: You must hate, He said *hate.* Hate my father, my mother, hate my wife [husband] and my children in order to follow Him.

R3: And of yourself?

R1: I am to take not thought of myself.

R2: He would not have you carry your own cross, would He?

R1: Yes, or I am unworthy to be called—disciple.

R2: He asked me, "Are you not a builder?"

R3: Of which you are.

R2: I pointed out the great tower project.

R1: Was He impressed?

R2: He simply said, "Did you not first consider the cost, even before the foundation was laid? Otherwise why start, if you cannot finish the task?"

R3: How is the project going?

R2: Will I finish the task?

R1: And of *your* kingdom what did He ask?

R3: It was a strange question. He asked, "Before battle do you seek counsel on the strength of your enemy, so that you know whether to rise up against them in strength or pursue terms of peace?"

R2: And for the war at hand?

R3: I need wise counsel.

(Pause)

R1: We must choose

R2: life,

R3: or death.

R1, R2: We are disciples

R3: or enemies.

R1: We are salt,

R2, R3: or we are tasteless and useless.

R3: He asks a great deal.

R2: Yes.

R1: He demands our very being.

R3: Have we counted the cost?

ALL: He who has ears, let him hear.

R1: And count the cost.

The Sacrifice of Love

by Barry Kolp

Cast:
BOB
SUSAN
JENNY
SEAN

Setting:
The dining room of a well-to-do suburban family. Two exits: one to the kitchen, and one to the stairs.

Props:
Set of everyday dishes
Set of good china
Serving bowl and spoon
Juice pitcher
Napkins and other tableware
Food as indicated (real or artificial)
Scrabble game
Dictionary
Pad of paper, pen
Calculator

Scene 1

(The family is eating dinner in the dining room. It is Thursday evening, one week before Thanksgiving.)

SUSAN: Bob, don't forget that both the kids have soccer practice tonight.

BOB: I know. But it doesn't start until 7:30. We've got plenty of time. *(To the children)* Do you have your homework done? I don't want a repeat performance of last week.

JENNY: I didn't get much today; I finished it in study hall.

SEAN: Mom and me worked on my spelling this afternoon.

JENNY: That's "Mom and I." Maybe we should have worked on grammar instead.

(BOB *laughs.)*

(They finish dinner, and SUSAN *and* JENNY *begin to clear the table.)*

JENNY: Mom, Dad, I was wondering something.

BOB: What's that, Jen?

JENNY: Could I get my own phone? I really need to have some privacy when I get phone calls, and there's no place in this house to be alone and talk in peace.

SUSAN: But can't you use the upstairs phone when you have a private call? That's what your father and I do.

JENNY: But the phone's in your room—and I'd like to have one in my room too. And you know how you complain about how I tie the line up with my calls. Besides, I never can be sure whether Sean is listening in on the kitchen extension or not. That's why I want a phone of my own.

BOB: Sean, you don't listen in on your sister's telephone conversation?

SEAN: No way, Dad. Why would I want to hear some ol' creepy girls talking, anyway?

JENNY *(exasperated):* Dad!

BOB: Sean, that's enough. Now, back to the point. I'm not convinced that you really need your own phone, Jenny. Anyway, the phone company would charge us every month for a second line. I'm not sure we can justify that kind of extra expense.

JENNY: But, Dad, all my friends have their own phones, and I don't see why I can't. It's not like I ask for so much around here.

BOB: What about that new CD player and speakers we got you just last month—and the 10 compact discs to go along with it?

JENNY: But that was for my birthday! It's hardly fair to bring that up.

SUSAN: Don't argue with your father, Jenny.

JENNY: I'm not arguing, Mother, but it *isn't* fair. Besides, Dad, if the money's the big hang-up, I can always do more baby-sitting to help pay for it.

BOB: The money's not the point. The point is your attitude. We're not here on earth to cater to your every whim. You could show a little more gratitude for all the nice things you *do* have. After all, it is almost Thanksgiving.

JENNY: All I do is ask one little question, and I get my head chewed off. It's just not fair. I don't see what I have to be grateful for, anyway. It's not like we live in a palace or anything.

BOB: Listen, young lady, your mother and I work hard for the money that pays for all the nice things we have around here. And although this house may not be a palace, it sure beats anything we had when we were your age.

JENNY: Oh, boy. Here we go again with the stories about your childhood in the backwoods.

SUSAN *(shocked):* Jennifer! How dare you talk like that to your father and me! I demand that you apologize immediately.

JENNY: Well, I'm *not* sorry and I *won't* apologize. *(She starts to leave the room.)*

BOB *(angry):* Hold on, there. Just who do you think you are—talking and acting like that? I won't have it, do you hear me? I just won't have it. Now, you sit down and listen to me. (JENNY *sits down. She pouts angrily.)* You're *not* going to have your own phone. Furthermore, you're *not* going to soccer practice tonight. You're going to go to your room and think about the way you've been acting. No TV, no music, no computer, no fun at all. And until you're ready to apologize—and *mean it*—you are *not* going to leave your room.

(JENNY's *anger deepens.)*

SEAN: Boy, Dad, she could be up there forever.

BOB: You stay out of this, young man, unless you want the same punishment. *(To* JENNY) Jenny, I meant it; go to your room—NOW! Susan, we've got to do *something* about this family's greed and lack of gratitude.

(A stunned silence follows this outburst. JENNY *leaves to go upstairs, sullenly.* SUSAN *and* SEAN *clear the table and exit to kitchen.* BOB *sits quietly at the table, deep in thought, as the curtain falls.)*

Scene 2

(BOB *and* SUSAN, *dressed in PJs and robes, are seated at the dining room table early on Friday morning. The table is set for breakfast. They are talking about the events of last night—and about the plan they devised. The children are still upstairs.)*

BOB: Well, Sue, I asked the Lord to forgive me for losing my temper last night, and I'm going to ask Jen to forgive me this morning—but I still don't think what she said was right.

SUSAN: I know, Bob, and I agree with you—she was out of line. But it seems like you've been awfully short-tempered with the children lately. Is something bothering you at work again?

BOB: Nothing specific. It's just that I'm not getting much satisfaction out of my work anymore. I feel sort of out of touch, out of control—I don't know, just not very happy there lately. Sue, I'm 40 years old, and I just can't see myself spending the rest of my life peddling hamburgers.

SUSAN: Sweetheart, I know how you feel. I always thought that by the time I was approaching 40, I'd be an accomplished writer. Instead, I'm a substitute English teacher, trying to pound the rules of grammar into the minds of junior high students. I feel like I'm wasting my talents. But we just have to trust Christ for the direction our lives take. After all, He is in control, right?

BOB: I have to be honest with you, Sue—I'm not as certain of that as I used to be. Sometimes, I feel like my life is so insignificant. I thought that being a Christian would make life seem so meaningful, but sometimes it all seems so frustrating.

SUSAN: Well, Bob, even though things may not be so great at work, you make a good living—plus you have a family that loves you. Not every man can say that.

BOB: Darling, I know that you and the children love me—I really do. But sometimes I feel like a failure as a father too. Just look at the way Jenny is turning out. The clothes she wants to wear, that garbage she listens to day and night, the boys she dates—and then that scene last night. Where did we go wrong, Sue? Have I been one of those absentee fathers?

SUSAN: Bob, don't be so hard on yourself. Jenny's just going through a rough time right now, though I must admit that I don't always understand her. She struggles with things that I just took for granted, growing up on the farm. But I know that Jenny's not unique. The other parents in our Sunday School class have the same doubts and fears about their own teenagers. And, comparing Jenny with some of my students at school, I'd say we're doing pretty well.

BOB: I guess every parent with teenagers must sometimes feel like we do. But I often wonder why Jenny can't be more like Sean. That boy's never given us a moment's grief.

SUSAN: Sean *is* a good boy—he's so good, sometimes he scares me. I wonder what *his* teen years will be like? And even though Jenny is frustrating sometimes, there are other times my heart just overflows with joy at being her mother. Raising children is like an emotional roller coaster—sometimes you're up, and sometimes you're down, but the ride is always exhilarating.

BOB: You're right, of course. I don't know what I'd do without you, Sue. You always manage to get me back on an even keel. *(They hug and kiss.)* And now, before the kids come downstairs, let's talk some more about the plan of action we agreed upon last night. Do you think they'll buy the idea at all?

SUSAN: Well, of course, they'll probably resist it. As children, we knew the value of things, since we had to learn to make do with so little. Our kids have always had everything they wanted, within reason. Bob, I think the discipline and self-restraint will be good for them. Like you said last night, we *do* have to do something about this family's lack of gratitude. After all, it'll be Thanksgiving soon. *(Looks at watch.)* The children should be down soon. I'll go get the cereal and juice.

(SUSAN *exits to kitchen. The children are heard coming down the stairs.)*

BOB *(calling to* SUSAN): Well, here they come. This should prove to be a very interesting breakfast.

Scene 3

(It is a little later on Friday morning. Everyone is wearing PJs and robes, seated around the table. The table is set with bowls, spoons, napkins, and juice glasses. There is a serving bowl of oatmeal and a pitcher of juice. SUSAN *dishes up the food.* JENNY *pours the juice.)*

BOB: It looks like we're ready to eat. Susan, would you please ask the blessing?

(Everyone bows their heads and folds their hands in an attitude of prayer.)

SUSAN: Dear Lord, we thank You for another day of life and for the many blessings You have given us. Thank You for the food we are about to eat, and for the family we have to share it with. Help each of us to know and do Your will today. In Jesus' name. Amen.

(They all say, "Amen.")

BOB: Jenny, there's something I need to say to you about last night. I'm really sorry about blowing my stack. I still think that you were out of line, but I had no right to lose my temper like that. I've asked Christ to forgive me, and now I'm asking for your forgiveness.

JENNY: Oh, Dad. I appreciate what you're doing—but *I'm* the one who needs to apologize. I shouldn't have spoken to you and Mom like that. Sometimes, when I get mad, I just can't seem to control myself. I'm really sorry. Can you and Mom forgive me?

SUSAN: Of course we can, Honey. Believe it or not, we remember what it's like to be a teenager. Let's just put it all behind us, all right?

JENNY: Sure! That sounds good to me.

BOB: It sounds good to me too.

SEAN: Hey, Mom?

SUSAN: What is it, Dear?

SEAN: This oatmeal's OK, but where's the rest of breakfast? I sure would like some waffles and sausage to go with this.

SUSAN: Well, Bob?

BOB *(to children):* I asked you to come down for breakfast early to tell you something. And the oatmeal's part of it.

JENNY: What is it, Dad?

BOB: Your mother and I have been talking about the problem that led to our argument last night. And we've come up with a plan that should help us get a handle on it.

JENNY: What problem are you talking about—asking for a phone of my own?

BOB: No, it's not that. Your desire for a private phone is just a symptom of the *real* problem.

SEAN: What's that?

SUSAN: Your dad and I believe that you two have failed to develop a proper sense of gratitude. And we feel at least partially responsible. We probably shouldn't have given you everything you asked for, but we wanted you to have the nice things that we never had.

BOB: And, honestly, we've probably been guilty of putting too much emphasis on material things ourselves. That's why we've come up with this plan.

JENNY: I'm not sure I like the sound of this.

BOB: After we tell you what we have planned, I'm sure you won't like it—but it's only for a week. What we plan to do—just for this next week—is try to live on 10 percent of our income. Since our combined yearly income is about $60,000, that means we'll try to live like people who make $6,000 a year.

JENNY: But nobody can live on that.

SUSAN: Sure they can, Jenny—that's about what your father and I made during college.

JENNY: But that was a long time ago, and you didn't have two children then.

BOB: You're right, though it wasn't *that* long ago. We'll have to get used to eating plainer food, like this oatmeal. And, all of our electronic gadgets will have to be put aside for the week, except the old black-and-white TV set, and maybe the old radio.

JENNY: You're kidding, right, Dad?

SUSAN: This is no joke and that's not all, Jenny. We're going to have to limit ourselves to three outfits apiece, and two pairs of shoes.

JENNY: You *can't* be serious! Three outfits for a whole week!

BOB: We're dead serious, Jen. And, furthermore, your allowances will be cut by 90 percent as well. If you two don't think you can make it on that amount, we have lots of extra chores that can be done around here. I think that our neighbors could probably use some willing workers too.

JENNY: It sounds like Sean and I have to make all the sacrifices. What are the two of you giving up?

SUSAN: Jenny, we'll be making sacrifices too. Your father will be taking the bus every day, as well as brown-bagging it to work. I'm not going to be using the microwave or the food processor. In fact, we'll be cutting back on foods like snacks, soft drinks, and red meat. And you and I will be going to the Suds and Duds Laundromat to do the clothes.

JENNY *(crying):* Mom, Dad—I think you're overreacting. This sure seems like a drastic punishment for asking for my own phone. Besides, I thought that was all forgiven—and forgotten.

(SUSAN *goes to* JENNY *and tries to comfort her with a hug.)*

BOB: Oh, Jenny, please try and understand—we're not punishing anyone. We think this experiment in a simple life-style will be beneficial to the whole family. *(To* SEAN) What about you, Sport? What do you think about the idea?

SEAN: I think it sounds neat, Dad—sort of like a camping trip, but staying at home. And I can take over Stevie's paper route, since he's got the flu.

JENNY: Well, *I* don't think it sounds neat at all, but it doesn't look like we have a choice, does it?

SUSAN: You're right. You *don't* really have a choice. Your dad and I have made a decision, and it's final. But, Jenny, can't you try and see it as an adventure, like your brother does?

JENNY: He sees *everything* as an adventure. But, since I don't have a choice, I'll do my best to live with it. I just hope the Lord gives me the strength to survive this next week.

BOB *(laughs):* Oh, Honey, I'm sure He will. And we're *all* going to need His help to see this through. It will be a big change for all of us. But one thing is certain—when this week is over, we'll all be more thankful for what He's given us. And that's the purpose of this whole experiment.

JENNY *(sarcastically):* Well, I guess I'd better go upstairs and pick out which of my three outfits I'm going to wear today.

SUSAN: That's the spirit!

(JENNY *exits to upstairs.* BOB *and* SEAN *help* SUSAN *clear the table, as the curtain falls.)*

Scene 4

(Everyone is gathered around the dining room table, eating Sunday dinner. The menu: meat loaf, instant mashed potatoes, canned green beans, bread, Jell-O, and Kool-Aid.)

JENNY: I thought Sunday dinner would be something special—not meat loaf. And these instant mashed potatoes are *terrible.*

SEAN: I think it's great, except for the orange Jell-O. Yuck!

SUSAN: Children, don't forget that we're trying to live as your father and I did in college. Back then, a meal like this would have seemed like a feast. And don't forget that there are many people who rarely have a hot meal at all. We should be thankful for what we have, instead of complaining.

BOB: Well, Sue, it's only been a few days—and you must admit that it is quite a change from our usual Sunday dinner.

SUSAN: I know that, Bob, but I'm doing the best I can with the food budget I have to work with.

BOB: Nobody's finding fault with you, Sweetheart. I guess it's just been a long weekend for all of us. Sean and I had a rough time delivering those huge papers this morning.

JENNY: What time did you have to get up, Dad?

BOB: FOUR A.M. To tell you the truth, I didn't get much out of the sermon this morning. I almost fell asleep twice.

JENNY *(laughing):* Sean *did* fall asleep. I thought I'd die laughing when he fell against Mrs. Johnson and started snoring.

SUSAN: Mrs. Johnson didn't think it was very funny—and I felt like crawling under the pew. Sean, I suppose it doesn't seem too much like an adventure anymore, does it?

SEAN: Oh, I'm OK, Mom. Those papers *did* get heavy, though. I don't see how Stevie does it. If it hadn't been for Dad's help, I'd still be delivering them!

BOB: Well, Son, I couldn't let you handle such a big job on your own. Regular papers are one thing—but the ones on Sunday are BEARS!

SUSAN: Jenny and I had quite an adventure at the Suds and Duds yesterday. The oddest-looking couple came in to do their clothes.

JENNY: Do you mean the guy with orange hair and the leather outfit and the girl with the spiked hair? I thought they looked rad.

BOB: I'm not sure, but does "rad" mean you approve of the way they looked?

JENNY: Oh, it's not for me, Dad. But I don't see anything wrong with it for other people. Not everybody has to look like us to be a good person.

SUSAN: It wasn't so much the way they looked as the way they acted that bothered me. The way they were kissing and touching each other—right there in the Laundromat. I thought it was disgusting.

JENNY: I thought it was gross, too, Mom. People who are really in love don't have to show off like that.

SUSAN: That's a very mature attitude, Jenny. Sometimes you surprise me.

JENNY: Oh, Mother, I'm not a child, after all. But I'm glad you've noticed that I *am* growing up. Thank you!

SUSAN: You're welcome, Honey. Sometimes it seems like you're becoming a young woman right before our eyes.

BOB: So, it sounds like you got the laundry done—and a free show too.

SUSAN: Bob, it's nothing to joke about. I never realized how much I took our washer and dryer for granted. It must be terrible to have to rely on the Laundromat all the time.

BOB: It seems to me that everyone is having a terrible time with our little experiment. And, I must admit that riding the bus is no picnic. Neither is eating a sandwich in my office while everyone else goes out to lunch. If you want to quit a few days early, I'll understand.

SUSAN: We *can't* give up on it this soon. Bob, we lived like this for over five years. I can stand it for a few more days. Can't you, kids?

SEAN: Sure!

JENNY: I guess so. If you guys did it for five years, I can do it for a week.

BOB: I'm proud of all of you. Even though we've only been trying this since Friday, I can already see a change for the better. I only have one request to make.

SUSAN: What's that, Bob?

BOB: Please, you and Jenny do the cleanup while Sean and I take a nap.

SEAN: Me, too, Dad! Those papers weighed a ton.

SUSAN *(laughing):* You big, strong men go take a little nap; Jenny and I can handle this.

(BOB *and* SEAN *wearily exit to upstairs, while* SUSAN *and* JENNY *begin clearing the table.)*

Scene 5

(The setting is the same: the dining room. It is Tuesday evening, after dinner. The family is seated around the table, playing Scrabble. It is very important for the opening dialogue to be done in a light, joking manner, or it will be misunderstood as an argument.)

SEAN: Is "quint" a word?

JENNY: Why don't you try it and see?

SEAN: Because you'll challenge me, and I'll lose my turn. You always do.

JENNY: I only challenge you and Dad because you both keep trying to use made-up words.

BOB: Hey! How did I get into this?

SUSAN: Because you *do* use words that only exist in your fertile imagination, Sweetheart.

BOB: Oh, yeah? Name two.

JENNY: What about "xerod"—and "yinka"? You know those aren't real words.

BOB: OK. I surrender. *(To* SEAN) I'd be careful, Sport. We're playing with a couple of Scrabble sharks here!

SEAN *(laughs):* I know, Dad. But I've got a good word, anyway. *Q-u-i-z—quiz. (He lays out the tiles.)* With the bonus points for having a double-letter space *and* a double word, my score is 64. What's my total now, Mom?

SUSAN: Let's see—227. Tell me, Son—how is it you can do all that in your head but have so much trouble with math in school?

SEAN: I don't know, Mom. I guess it depends on whether it matters to me or not. Anyway, it's your turn, Sis.

JENNY: All I can come up with is *now* for 6 points. *(She places the tiles on the board.)* Where do I stand, Mom?

SUSAN: You have 152 points, Jenny. (JENNY *groans.)* It's your turn, Bob.

BOB: Building on Sean's *z,* here's my word—*z-o-r-i-l, zoril.*

SEAN: What does *zoril* mean, Dad?

BOB: I knew somebody would ask me that, Son. It's a skunklike animal that lives in South America. Does anyone want to challenge that?

SUSAN: I have some trouble accepting that definition, Bob; it's a little too pat. So I guess I'm challenging it.

BOB: Well, look it up.

(SUSAN *does—and discovers that it IS a word.)*

SUSAN: I hate to admit it, but you're right. How did you know that word, Bob?

BOB: I guess the old man still has a few tricks up his sleeve, doesn't he? Since I used all my tiles, the game's over. Let's see—my word was worth 42. Adding in the bonus for using all my tiles, plus the value of all your left-over letters, gives me 104 points. Now, what are our final scores?

SUSAN: Your total is 224. Jenny has 147, and I have 183. Sean wins with 225.

BOB: Why, you little scamp. How did you manage that?

SEAN: I guess the young man still has a few tricks up his sleeve, doesn't he? *(Everyone laughs and begins clearing the board.)*

SUSAN: This has been such a pleasant evening, without all the usual rushing around, like chickens with their heads cut off. I don't know why we don't do this more often.

BOB: I guess we just let ourselves get too busy, Sue. Somehow the important things, like time with the family, get pushed aside. Activities that are more urgent or that are expected of us tend to take center stage.

SUSAN: You're right on target there, Bob. Ever since we've started our little experiment, and I cut back on my television viewing, I've found more time for the really important things. In fact, I've starting writing again. I'm working on an article describing our plan. It's really going well—and it helps me put what we're doing in its proper perspective. I'm thinking of submitting the article to the *Herald of Holiness* or some other Christian magazine—or maybe even the *Ladies Home Journal.*

BOB: That's great, Sue! I *knew* you had it in you!

JENNY: I know where you're coming from, too, Mom. The things that seemed to matter so much a few days ago—like following the latest trends, or hanging out with the "right people"—somehow they don't seem so important anymore. Don't get me wrong; I still want to look good, but I don't think I have to look like a model to do that.

BOB: Is that really our Jen—the clothes horse—talking? But I know what you mean. This experiment has helped me a lot. Eating out last night at our store in the mall was a real revelation. I realize now that I've been out of touch with the people who eat in our restaurants. Good food at a good price, in a pleasant place, served by friendly people—that's what will make folks come to our stores; not fancy advertising campaigns, contests, or snappy slogans. I've got some new ideas that should help the company improve both its sales and the value of what we sell.

SEAN: And I'm having fun delivering the newspapers. I do my best to hit each porch without stopping my bike. It's sort of like playing Lazer Tag on wheels. Plus, it feels good to give people something they need—and get paid for it too.

SUSAN: It seems to me that our little experiment is having some unexpected benefits. Maybe we should have tried something like this a long time ago.

BOB: I know one thing: when we go to prayer meeting tomorrow night, the Marshall family will have something *worth* testifying about.

SUSAN: Perhaps we should share our idea with some of the other families at church, Bob; we can't be the only ones who have a problem with our priorities. It's all too easy to let our possessions possess us, instead of the other way around. Even Christians aren't exempt from struggling with this. Maybe what we've learned about ourselves could help someone else.

BOB: I think you're right, Darling. If it's all right with all of you, I think I'll tell the pastor about what we've discovered; he'll know the best way to share our idea with others. *(The others agree.)* And now, it's getting sort of late. You'd better finish your homework while Mom and I get things ready for family devotions.

(The children exit to upstairs, while BOB *and* SUSAN *get out the Bible and other devotional materials, including several hymnbooks.)*

Scene 6

(The family is seated for breakfast, dressed in their nightclothes—except SEAN, *who is fully dressed. It is Thanksgiving morning. They are already eating—oatmeal, again, with toast.)*

SEAN: Mom, why's everybody up so early? I had to get up to deliver my papers, but I thought you would all sleep late, since it's a holiday.

SUSAN: Normally we would, Sean, but today's a special day. We have a lot to do.

JENNY: You mean getting the turkey and all the trimmings ready, right, Mom?

SUSAN: That, plus a whole lot more.

JENNY: Like what?

BOB: Remember the food baskets we all worked on after church last night? Well, I'm going out with several of the other men to deliver them this morning.

SEAN: Oh, boy, Dad. Can I go with you? I won't get in the way, or anything, and I can help carry the bags.

BOB *(smiling):* Sure, Sport, you can go. But I think the bags might be a little heavy for you.

SEAN: Not after lugging those papers around this week.

BOB *(laughing):* You may be right. OK, Son you come with me—and I'll help *you* carry the bags of food.

SUSAN: And, Jenny, I'm going to need your help this morning to get our Thanksgiving dinner ready.

JENNY: OK, Mom. But why are we going to fix it so early, instead of working on it this afternoon?

BOB: Because this afternoon, your mother and I won't be here. We volunteered to help serve Thanksgivng dinner down at My Father's House.

SEAN: But I thought Grandma and Grandpa lived in Indiana.

SUSAN *(laughing gently):* No, Sean, your dad wasn't talking about his parents. My Father's House is the name of the emergency shelter and soup kitchen sponsored by the ministerial association. The company your dad works for donates food to them, and the pastor is on its Board of Directors.

SEAN: Oh, I understand now. But why are the people who go there only getting soup for Thanksgiving?

JENNY: Soup kitchen is just the name for a place that gives handouts to bums, Sean.

SUSAN *(shocked):* Jenny, that's no way to describe either the people who receive our help or the Christian love that it's given in.

JENNY: Well, I'm sorry, Mom, but I just don't have much sympathy for people who are too lazy to work for a living. After all, doesn't the Bible say, "God helps them who help themselves"?

BOB: First of all, that expression is not in the Bible. The essence of the gospel is that God, through Christ, helped us when we were helpless. And, secondly, I'm beginning to wonder if you really understand what we've been trying to do this week. Can't you see that people who are poor are just as valuable in God's sight as the richest man on earth?

JENNY: I'm sorry for what I said, Dad. I didn't really mean it. This has just been a tough week. The house is so cold with the thermostat turned back, I'm thoroughly sick of oatmeal, I'm tired of wearing the same three outfits—and I would *love* to be able to take a *long,* hot shower. I know I sound like a big crybaby, but I'm just not used to living this way.

SUSAN: Jenny, listen to me. I understand how you feel. I've felt the same way myself this week. It hasn't been easy for any of us. But, you need to imagine how it would feel to live like this—every day, every week, every month. Try to put yourself in their place, Honey. How would *you* feel? It's no wonder some folk just give up.

JENNY: I think I'm beginning to understand, Mom. Let me ask you something.

SUSAN: Sure, go ahead.

JENNY: Do you think it would be all right if Sean and I went with you and Dad to work in the soup kitchen this afternoon? I really would like to help.

BOB: There's no problem with that. And, Jenny, I want you to know something: I'm very proud of you for volunteering to help. *(They hug.)* And now, I guess you'd better go change; we have a big day ahead of us. Sean, it's our turn to do the dishes.

SEAN: Are you sure? *(Pauses)* OK, Dad, you're the boss.

(SEAN *and* BOB *clear the table as the ladies exit to upstairs.)*

Scene 7

(The family is seated at the table, which is set with fine china and a turkey dinner with all the trimmings. The family is dressed in "nice" casual clothes. They are already eating, but JENNY *isn't eating very much.)*

SUSAN: Jenny, you're just playing with your food. Don't you feel well?

JENNY: Oh, I feel all right physically, Mom. I just can't stop thinking about the people there at My Father's House. They seemed so sad, and lonely, and desperate. Oh, Mom, Dad, how can people live like that?

BOB: Life's a real struggle under those circumstances. I'm just glad we were able to help them have a nice Thanksgiving, at least.

SEAN: I just wish it was Thanksgiving every day.

SUSAN: Why, so that you could eat turkey all the time?

SEAN: No, Mom, so that those people would get help all the time.

BOB: Well, "Out of the mouth of babes." You know, Sue, the way the children are feeling just confirms what I've been thinking.

SUSAN: What's that, Dear?

BOB: That we should cut our spending level permanently and share some of our blessings with others. Last night, when I talked to the pastor, he told me what John Wesley had to say about Christians and their money. Wesley's advice was: "*Make* all you can; *save* all you can; and *give away* all you can." I think that's good advice, don't you?

SUSAN: Yes, I do—but there's no way we can live at this level all the time. We have bills, the mortgage payment, all sorts of financial obligations. We just can't do it, Bob.

BOB: Oh, don't misunderstand me. I wasn't thinking about trying to do that. But I think we *can* cut our expenses by about 10 percent, and thus have more money to give to worthy causes.

JENNY: That sounds like a great idea, Dad. I'm willing to do without some things if it will help people like we met this afternoon. I guess I really don't need to get new shoes or jeans as often as I say I do. And, if I do more baby-sitting, I won't need as much allowance.

SEAN: Me either, Dad. Maybe I could get a paper route of my own and give some of the money to the emergency shelter.

SUSAN: Now, that's the spirit, Sean and Jenny. If it's all right with everybody, we can make some of the things we've been doing this week permanent. For instance, we can save quite a bit by not eating meat at every meal—and by not eating out so often. And, if I'm just a little more careful about things, like looking for bargains and using coupons, I'm sure we can cut our living expenses way back.

BOB: I think I can get into a car pool at work. That would save a lot of wear and tear on the car. We can turn the thermostats back, all year round, and take shorter showers. There are lots of other ways to really cut back on our utility bills. And I suppose I can make do with my old power tools for another year. And, kids, just wait till you taste some of the special dishes your mom used to make when we were in college—yum-yum! *(They all laugh.)*

SUSAN *(kiddingly):* I thought you *liked* my tuna surprise! *(Seriously)* It really sounds like we're all getting into the spirit of living more simply. I'm so proud of all of you! Now, is everyone finished with dinner? *(They are.)* Good. Let's clear the table and begin to write down some ideas on how to give away all this money we're going to save.

(They take the dishes to the kitchen. BOB *gets a pad of paper and printing calculator from the hutch.)*

BOB: Let's see—a 10 percent cut in spending would free up about $6,000 a year for helping other people. Increasing our regular giving to the church to a total of 15 percent would use about half of that. Now, how should we divide up the rest?

JENNY: We definitely want to help My Father's House. How does $50.00 a month for that sound?

(Everyone agrees. SUSAN *writes it on the pad.)*

BOB *(using calculator):* OK, I've got it entered. You know, I was talking to the missionary president last night at church. She said that several families give a yearly offering for missions that equals two weeks' salary. That would be a $1,000 increase for us. Is that all right with everyone?

(They agree. SUSAN *writes it down.* BOB *enters it.)*

SUSAN: What about the church's Compassionate Ministries Fund, for the food pantry and other needs? I'd like to support it more regularly. I think $50.00 a month would be fair; all right?

(They all agree. SUSAN *writes it down.)*

BOB: We're up to nearly $5,000. Sean, do you have any suggestions?

SEAN: What about sponsoring a poor child from some other country, like we see on TV all the time?

BOB: That's a great idea, Son. I think it would run about $25.00 a month, through a Christian relief agency. *(They enter the figure.)* And I think it would be good to support a group called Habitat for Humanity that the pastor told me about. They build good-quality, simple homes and sell them to poor people with a no-interest loan. There's a chapter right here in town.

SUSAN: That's a wonderful idea, Sweetheart. How much support do you think we should give them?

BOB: Oh, $25.00 a month sounds about right to me. *(They enter this item.)* Let's see, that leaves about $500 a year to share with others.

JENNY: I think we ought to start a scholarship fund at the church college with it. We could ask them to give the money to a student from an inner-city background.

BOB: That's an excellent choice, Honey. The poor don't really want a handout; what they want is a hand up to a better life. Education is one of the best ways I know to accomplish that. Just look at where your mother and I came from. Without help, we certainly wouldn't be where we are today. Why, I remember times growing up—

SUSAN *(interrupting and laughing):* Oh, Bob, not another "backwoods story," as Jenny would say.

BOB *(chagrined):* All right—no war stories. I was just trying to make a point about how education can help.

JENNY: We get your drift, Dad. And, we agree with you. You know, I feel a whole lot better than I did when we started eating dinner. Helping other people isn't really a sacrifice—if you love them, like Jesus did.

SUSAN: That's exactly right, Jen; and I hope we all remember that when we begin to feel the pinch of living more simply.

JENNY: Oh, Mother, I won't forget.

SEAN: Me, either. This week *really* has been an adventure, hasn't it?

BOB: It certainly has. And, you know, I think the lessons we've learned will make our traditional Thanksgiving hymn very special this year. *(To* SUSAN*)* Sweetheart, will you get the hymnbooks out?

(Each one places a hymnbook on the table in front of them. They join hands and sing verses 1, 3, and 4 of "For the Beauty of the Earth.")

"For the Beauty of the Earth"

For the beauty of the earth,
For the glory of the skies,
For the love which from our birth
Over and around us lies,
Lord of all, to Thee we raise
This our hymn of grateful praise.

For the joy of human love,
Brother, sister, parent, child;
Friends on earth, and friends above;
For all gentle thoughts and mild;
Lord of all, to Thee we raise
This our hymn of grateful praise.

For Thy Church that evermore
Lifteth holy hands above,
Offering up on every shore
Her pure sacrifice of love,
Lord of all, to Thee we raise
This our hymn of grateful praise.

THE END

For Where Your Treasure Is

Readers Theater

by Bette Dale Moore

ONE: Girl
TWO: Boy
THREE: Girl
FOUR: Boy
FIVE: Girl

THREE: The text for today's message is taken from the Book of Exodus. And the Lord told Moses:

FOUR: "From what you have, take an offering for the Lord."

FIVE: ". . . of gold,"

TWO: "silver,"

ONE: "and bronze" (35:5).

FOUR: "All who are *skilled* among you are to come and make everything the Lord has commanded" (35:10).

ONE: "[Then] everyone who was willing"

TWO: "and whose heart moved him"

ONE: "came and brought . . . to the Lord freewill offerings . . . morning after morning" (35:21, 29; 36:3).

THREE: "[Until finally] the people were restrained from bringing more,"

TWO and FOUR: "because what they already had"

ONE and FIVE: "was more than enough"

ALL: "to do all the work" (36:6-7).

TWO: And they all lived happily ever after.

ONE and THREE: What?

FIVE: That's not part of the story.

TWO: No. But it should be.

ONE: It should be?

TWO: Yes, because it's a fairy tale.

FOUR: In the Bible? That's impossible!

THREE: Fairy tales are make-believe,

ONE: and God's Word is true.

TWO: But, whoever heard of people being asked to STOP giving? Especially in a church? If that's not a fairy tale, I don't know what I'd call it.

THREE: I'd call it truth.

FOUR: I'd call it reality.

FIVE: I'd call it obedience.

TWO *(awed):* All that? Just from giving? What's so special about giving?

(All speak rapidly.)

ONE: Give.

THREE: Gave.

FIVE: Have given.

(All speak a little slower.)

FOUR: Bequeath.

THREE: Offer.

TWO: Dedicate.

(They speak slower still.)

THREE: To bestow freely.

FOUR: To deliver.

FIVE: To devote.

ONE: Thank you, class, for that timely definition. Now, if you will all take out your Sunday School quarterlies and *(turns to page)*—

(FIVE *waves hand.)*

FIVE: Teacher?

ONE: Yes, Pam, what is it?

FIVE: Last week, we studied about the wealth of the Lord.

TWO: "The earth is the Lord's,"

THREE: "and everything in it,"

FOUR: "the world,"

TWO, THREE, and FOUR: "and all who live in it."

FIVE: Psalm 24, verse 1.

ONE: Very good.

FIVE: But, if God owns everything, why is He always so broke?

ONE: Pardon me?

FIVE: Practically every time you turn around, the church is taking an offering.

THREE: Thanksgiving.

TWO: Easter.

FOUR: Christmas.

TWO: Building Fund.

FOUR: Home Missions.

THREE: Debt Reduction.

FIVE: And besides all that, there's always . . .

TWO, THREE and FOUR: Tithing!

FIVE: Seems to me that if God would invest the money we gave Him last month,

FOUR: in stocks and bonds,

THREE: in futures;

TWO: in some up-and-coming company,

FIVE: then He wouldn't always be begging for more. *(Happily)* Isn't that a great idea? . . . Isn't it?

(ONE *and* TWO *shake heads and look down.)*

THREE: God's not begging for money.

TWO: Why should He?

ONE: He already owns everything.

FOUR *(with authority):* "I have no need of a bull from your stall or of goats from your pens, for every animal of the forest is mine, and the cattle on a thousand hills" (Psalm 50:9).

FIVE: God doesn't need our gifts.

THREE: But *we* need to give.

TWO: "Give to the one who asks you" (Matthew 5:42).

ONE: "Sell your possessions and give to the poor. . . ."

FIVE: "For where your treasure is, there your heart will be also" (Luke 12:33-34).

FOUR: Treasure?

THREE: Yes. Those things that we value above all else.

FIVE: That which we hold dearest.

ONE and TWO: Our most prized possessions.

THREE: When money becomes "treasure,"

ONE: it also becomes Lord,

FIVE: Master,

TWO: Ruler of the heart.

THREE: "No servant can serve two masters. . . ."

TWO: "You cannot serve both God and Money" (Luke 16:13).

FOUR: So, how do I keep from treasuring money?

ONE: Don't hold on to it.

TWO: "Be generous."

THREE: "Willing to share."

ALL except FOUR: GIVE.

TWO: "In this way [you] will lay up treasure" for yourself in heaven,

FIVE: Taking hold "of the life"

ONE: "that is truly LIFE"! (1 Timothy 6:18-19).

FOUR: OK. If spiritual treasures are what I should have, then I'll give all my money to the poor. And I promise never to touch another penny—as long as I live.

THREE: I think you've missed the point.

FOUR: I have?

THREE: It's not wrong to have money.

ONE: It's simply wrong to treasure it.

TWO: "The love of money is a root of . . . evil" (1 Timothy 6:10).

FIVE: Not money itself.

FOUR: OK. Have it your way. I'll keep all my money then.

TWO: No! Don't do that.

THREE: Money is intended to be used as a tool,

ONE: an instrument for accomplishing God's purpose.

FIVE: To deny its usefulness is to hinder the work of God.

TWO: God owns the cattle on a thousand hills,

THREE: but He needs us to distribute the beef!

ONE *(with authority):* "'Bring the whole tithe into the storehouse, that there may be food in my house.' says the Lord Almighty, 'and see if I will not . . . pour out so much blessing that you will not have room enough for it'" (Malachi 3:10).

FIVE: But beware of false teaching regarding this.

TWO *(aggressively):* Brother and sisters, if you are writhing in the throes of poverty; if you are teetering on the brink of financial destruction—then hear what I have to say! The Lord does not want us to be poor. He has told us: "Give, and it will be given to you" (Luke 6:38). If you want more, then you've got to give more!

ONE: Do not be deceived.

FOUR: "Men of corrupt mind . . . have been robbed of the truth and . . . think that godliness is a means to financial gain" (1 Timothy 6:5).

THREE: God does not reward righteousness with wealth.

FIVE: Godliness has its own reward:

TWO: the fruit of the Spirit.

ONE: Communion with God.

TWO: Heavenly treasures!

FIVE: The ability to make money is simply a gift of God.

THREE *(bitterly):* Well, I've lived all my life for the Lord, and I can tell ya for sure that I ain't been gifted with makin' money. I guess maybe the Lord likes to give His gifts to some folks more than He likes to give 'em to others.

FOUR *(gently):* Don't you feel you've been given a gift?

THREE: From the looks of my bank account, I'd say, "Obviously not!"

TWO: But, what about the other gifts?

ONE: Serving.

FIVE: Teaching.

ONE: Encouraging.

TWO: To name just a few.

THREE: What good can any of those things do without hard, cold cash?

FIVE: Your heart is with the wrong treasure, my friend.

FOUR: The love of money has kept you from discovering your true gift,

ONE: and robbed you of the joy of giving.

TWO: No gift is better than another,

FIVE: for they all come from God.

THREE: "If a man's gift . . . is contributing to the needs of others, let him give generously" (Romans 12:6, 8).

FOUR: But if you are not financially gifted, do not use that as an excuse for miserliness.

ONE: We are all expected to give . . .

ALL: . . . from what we have.

TWO: Resources.

THREE: Time.

FOUR: Talent.

ONE: I'd like to use my talents for the Lord, but I'm afraid I'm just not good enough.

FIVE: I know exactly how you feel. There are so many others who are better than me. I'm ashamed to even offer to help.

TWO: I wish I had a talent. You can sing *(to* ONE), and you're artistic *(to* FIVE), but I can't do anything.

THREE: "We [all] have different gifts, according to the grace given us" (Romans 12:6).

FOUR: If you haven't discovered your gift yet,

THREE: perhaps you've been looking in the wrong place.

FOUR: Don't give up.

TWO: Keep on looking.

THREE: Find your gift.

FOUR: Develop it.

FIVE: Use it.

TWO: And don't be concerned about whether it's good enough or not.

FOUR: "For if the willingness is there, the gift is acceptable according to what one has,"

TWO: "not according to what he does not have" (2 Corinthians 8:12).

THREE *(self-righteously):* I realize how important it is to give. I've taught a Sunday School class for 30 years. I tell you, I've given to those kids until it hurts!

ONE: Well, don't stop there!

TWO: If you've only given until it hurts,

FIVE: then you haven't given enough.

FOUR: Give until all heaven breaks loose, and you're filled with the joyous blessings of God!

TWO: Remember the children of Israel?

THREE: They willingly gave from what they had:

ONE: Gold.

TWO: Silver.

THREE: Bronze.

FOUR: Their skills.

FIVE: Their time.

TWO: And what was their reward?

ONE: A holy covenant with God himself;

THREE: a treasure that would endure throughout eternity.

FOUR: All that we think we possess—

ONE: Our riches,

THREE: Our talents,

FIVE: Our time—

FOUR: are not really ours at all;

TWO: for everything that we have belongs to the Father.

ONE: We are but stewards of His great wealth.

FIVE: So when the Spirit of God moves within our hearts, telling us to use our gifts for His glory,

THREE: we should do so!

TWO: Freely.

ONE: With simplicity.

FOUR: Regularly.

FIVE: Cheerfully.

THREE: God himself has set the example, for "he gave his one and only Son (John 3:16),

ONE: His most prized possession,

FIVE: His greatest treasure:

ALL: Jesus Christ,

FOUR: "in whom are hidden all the treasures of wisdom and knowledge" (Colossians 2:3).

TWO: And now, we hold this unspeakable Treasure within our own bodies of clay—

GIRLS: Christ in us.

ONE: And it is His light that illumines our spiritual gifts,

FIVE: enabling us to give to Him,

THREE: the One who has given so much to us.

GIRLS: This is truth.

BOYS: This is reality.

ALL: This Treasure.

(All sing.)

Stewardship of God's Creation

Scripture Arrangement for Responsive Reading

In the beginning God created the heavens and the earth.

The earth is the Lord's, and everything in it, the world, and all who live in it.

For he founded it upon the seas and established it upon the waters.

He set the earth on its foundations; it can never be moved.

And God saw that it was good.

Praise the Lord, O my soul. . . . You are clothed with splendor and majesty.

God said, "Let there be light," and there was light.

He wraps himself in light as with a garment; he stretches out the heavens like a tent.

And God saw that it was good.

He makes the clouds his chariot and rides on the wings of the wind.

God said, "Let the water under the sky be gathered to one place, and let dry ground appear."

He makes grass grow for the cattle, and plants for man to cultivate—bringing forth food from the earth.

And God saw that it was good.

The trees of the Lord are well watered. . . . There the birds make their nests.

God said, "Let the water teem with living creatures, and let birds fly above the earth. . . . Let the land produce living creatures according to their kinds."

The moon marks off the seasons, and the sun knows when to go down. . . . And all the beasts of the forest prowl.

And God saw that it was good.

How many are your works, O Lord! In wisdom you made them all; the earth is full of your creatures.

God said, "Let us make man in our image, in our likeness."

"And let them rule over the fish of the sea and the birds of the air, over the livestock, over all the earth, and over all the creatures that move along the ground."

And God saw that it was good.

May the glory of the Lord endure forever.

May the Lord rejoice in his works.

(Unison) Praise the Lord, O my soul. Praise the Lord.

Genesis 1:1; Psalm 24:1-2; Psalm 104:5; Genesis 1:10; Psalm 104:1; Genesis 1:3; Psalm 104:2-3; Genesis 1:9; Psalm 104:14, 16-17; Genesis 1:20, 24; Psalm 104:19-20, 24; Genesis 1:26; Psalm 104:31, 35

The Conversion of Dastardly Dan
or
How Shall We Pay the Mortgage?

by Diana P. Ludwick

This play can be performed in four ways: with full scenery and props; arena style; as a radio drama; or as an entertaining compromise between radio and stage—as shown below.

Props

Two old-fashioned radio microphones on tall stands set about 10 feet apart. Mikes should resemble studio mikes such as RKO.
A reading stand or podium behind each mike
Five stools behind right microphone
One stool behind left microphone
One 1940s vintage radio
White silk hats and capes (two each)
Black silk hat and cape
Ladies wear turn-of-the-century-style blouses or dresses

Characters:

ANNOUNCER
MERRY MARIE
SWEET SUE
RELUCTANT RUTH
FEARLESS PHIL FEATHERWEIGHT
DASTARDLY DAN DILLINGER; AKA, THE VILLAIN

ANNOUNCER: Before the days of television, there was another kind of drama. In these plays, you had to use your imagination; and when the actors were very good and the sound effects were right, you could be transported to another world—a world where . . . anything . . . could happen.
As the lights dim, you will see yourself in your own living room. But, there is no television set, no VCR. Your only entertainment comes from a small box like this one. *(Spotlight focuses on old radio.)*

(Spot goes out on radio and comes up on three actors around mike on right. The "Lone Ranger" tape is being played, and the three actors say, ". . . and with a mighty shout of 'Hi Ho Silver' . . .")

DIRECTOR *(loudly whispers from offstage):* Psst, that's the wrong one! . . . Just go on!

ANNOUNCER: You are in a little chapel in Smallsville, U.S.A. Three ladies are sitting around a quilting frame making tiny stitches in a large project. Merry Marie is speaking.

(ANNOUNCER*'s spot goes black.)*

MERRY MARIE: Oh, Sweet Sue, what shall we do? The roof leaks, the floor squeaks, the window slips, the paint chips, the mortgage is due, and I'm so blue.

SWEET SUE: There, there, don't despair. Your husband, the good pastor, Fearless Phil Featherweight, will think of something.

RELUCTANT RUTH *(aside to audience):* He always does.

(Sound effect of a door closing is heard. FEARLESS PHIL *joins the ladies.)*

FEARLESS PHIL *(wears white top hat and cape):* Can this be my Merry Marie? Have no fear, my dear, for I am here!

MERRY MARIE: But, I was just telling Sweet Sue and Reluctant Ruth that the roof leaks, and the floor squeaks,

SWEET SUE: The window slips and the paint chips,

RELUCTANT RUTH: And the mortgage is due.

RUTH, SUE, and MARIE *(simultaneously):* And we're so blue. *(All cry.)* Boohoo.

(Sound effect of a door closing is heard. THE VILLAIN *joins the group. He wears a black top hat and cape.)*

VILLAIN: A good afternoon to you, ladies . . . and to you, good Reverend. *(He tips his hat.)* But, what are these? Tears? You couldn't be worried about losing this place. Why, the roof leaks and the floor squeaks, the window slips and the paint chips, the mortgage is due and I'M NOT SO BLUE! *(He laughs an evil laugh and disappears. Door closes loudly.)*

FEARLESS PHIL: There, there, ladies. Come, let us be gone to the parsonage. Things look grim, but, we'll not give in!

(The light goes to the ANNOUNCER.)

ANNOUNCER: And now, a word from our sponsor.
Do you have yellow, stained teeth? Hide that ugly smile with Brite-Glo Toothpolish. It will cover those dirty pearlies with the day-glo color of your choice! Available in chartreuse, neon yellow, and hot pink.
Now, back to our drama.

FEARLESS PHIL: Oh, that Dastardly Dan Dillinger! Why, that mean, monstrous, mealymouthed, miserly penny-pincher!

(Ladies gasp after each expletive.)

SWEET SUE: Well . . . well . . . I think he's kind of cute!

(FEARLESS PHIL, MERRY MARIE, *and* RELUCTANT RUTH *are all taken aback in shock! Lights go out.)*

(New scene. VILLAIN *at his own mike in an aside to the audience.)*

VILLAIN: At last, at last, I've forced their hand. I've got their church and I've got their land! Ah, suppose there are those who would help my foes. Perhaps, t'would be wise to wear a disguise; to sneak over at night, stay out of sight, and learn, firsthand, the plot of their plan. *(Laughs evilly and moves, with ear cocked, to side of others.)*

(The light follows, and second light is turned back on to show group at right mike. Short pause.)

FEARLESS PHIL *(snaps his fingers and shouts):* I've got it! We'll have a bake sale!

SWEET SUE: Oh, what a wonderful idea!

MERRY MARIE: An inspired idea!

RELUCTANT RUTH: We'll invite everyone from town, and I'll bake some cookies, golden brown.

SWEET SUE: I'll bake a cherry pie that's not too sour.

FEARLESS PHIL: I'll set up tables on the hour.

VILLAIN *(to audience):* And I'll put a whole jar of ants in the flour!

(Spotlights go out. There is a short pause, then one spot comes back to show the VILLAIN *only.)*

VILLAIN: I'm here in their kitchen with the flour and my jar of ants. Ha-ha-ha. I'll take care of Reverend Smarty-pants!

(Second spot comes on to show others.)

FEARLESS PHIL: Aha! I've caught you in the act! Put down that jar and drop that sack!

VILLAIN: Curses, foiled again.

FEARLESS PHIL: All right, Villain, this is more than I can abide. Let's roll up our sleeves and step outside.

MERRY MARIE: Stop! Stop! He is an evil man, it's true. But this is the wrong thing to do.

SWEET SUE: She's right, a pastor really shouldn't fight. But, someone here must show the light. A pie in the face seems just right!

(Sound effect of a "splot" is heard.)

VILLAIN: Why, Sweet Sue! You're not only pretty, you've got a temper too! Oh, what a wicked man I've been. Sweet Sue, if I repent, will you give your consent to marry me and forever be my one and only love?

SWEET SUE: Oh, yes, my dearest Dan. Somehow, I always knew God could work in you. But, what about the mortgage? What will you do?

VILLAIN: My life is turned around; you may burn the mortgage. *(Changes to white hat and cape with a flourish.)* I wonder if I can help the orphan's home with its shortage?

SWEET SUE: My hero!

FEARLESS PHIL: Well, now that the mortgage is clear, we'll have enough from the bake sale to fix the roof that leaks,

MERRY MARIE: And the floor that squeaks,

SWEET SUE: And the window that slips,

RELUCTANT RUTH: And the paint that chips,

FEARLESS PHIL: Yes, yes, that's what we'll do, and there'll be enough left over for a wedding too!

ALL *(clap and cheer):* Yea, yea, hooray! *(Over and over again. Lights on, actors take a bow.)*

Sarah Mae's Offering

A Monologue Circa 1910

by Gail Blanton

Character:
SARAH MAE: a mountain woman

Scene:
A country town church sanctuary in the year 1910

Props:
Mason jar of green beans
Paper bag
Hat

(SARAH MAE *carries a Mason jar of green beans concealed in a paper bag. She enters front of sanctuary and ascends steps to the stage, looking at everything in awe, perhaps touching walls or objects.)*

Howdy. Ooooowee, you-uns *(pronounced "yuns")* got you a fancy church down here in *(name of your city).* I ain't never seen nothin' to beat it. Bet they ain't got nothin' no finer thant this plumb down to Knoxville. Hey, you-uns don't mind if I take my shoes off, do you? *(As she continues, she sets the bag down and leaves it until the end, and takes off her shoes and leaves them also.)* It wus a long walk from where I live, and that sun is hot. Twudn't so bad till it got up over Old English. That's the second peak over behind here, y'know, and I live purt near the top—jest right below Augur Rock. That's a right fur piece—yessir, a right fur piece. I don't ever git down to town much. Maybe if some of my kin got a wagonload of wood to sell, I ken hitch a ride in an' find out what's goin' on. Why, it musta been spring of the year afore I knowed Mr. Taft had been voted in Presydent last November. Me and my brother George likes to come down sometimes to see can we git a look at one of the auty mobiles. Seen one oncet or twicet. Not countin' them few what's out there in the churchyard today. That's why I wus a little late comin' in. I was jest lookin' at 'em up close—and I touched one.

But that ain't why I come here. No indeed. Well, I reckon you're wonderin'. And it wus kind of yur preacher to let me testyfy first. I know all of you'ns got a lot to say, but he said I could say my piece and git on back, beings I gotta walk so fur. Well, I come here today to give an offerin'. See, to me it's a real special offerin', and I wanted to give it in a real church-house. I mean, we got us a church a ways up the mountain, but it's a schoolhouse 'cepting on the Sabbath. Ain't got no altar or nothin'. I ken worship in it, but it ain't quite right somehow, after all these years. I set in that little buildin' the whole six years of my education *(pronounced "edgycation"),* and I always feel kindly like a youngun in there—like I never growed up. Like I oughta write all my sins down on my slate or somethin'. Offerin's layin' up there on the desk like an apple fer the teacher. It just ain't fittin'.

Ooooo, my maw wouldn't stood for none of that kinda talk when she was alive. She said any place could be holy ground. And jest about all of God's good ground wus holy to her. Y'know, she could love stuff right outa the ground. Shucks, she could nurse corn till it wus full as a fat baby; mother her a brood of cucumbers or tomaters like she wus the vine itself. Kentucky Wonders climbed her poles like a black snake up an apple tree. She put up mess after mess of beans and thangs in fruit jars and laid 'em by in the shed. Row after row, as God prospered her. But the first in ever' 10 wus her tithe. She took it to the schoolhouse on Sunday to hep the Lord feed the needy. Seemed like a purty good idear to me, but then I didn't really think on it much. It was jest a way uv life. 'Sides, there wus always plenty left fer us. I loved my maw's green beans better'n anybody *(chuckles).* Et mor'n anybody too. Never tasted nothin' no finer in my life than my maw's green beans. Maybe there wus somethin' about that ground.

What ground my maw didn't garden she walked, birthin' babies, and I figger them wus holy walks. Midwifed ever' baby born on the mountain fer years. Never lost but one twin—two if you count the other twin. Its mother never lived to birth it, and it died inside her. Thing is, the onliest mother and baby my maw ever lost wus her own blood. That wus my sister Janie. Purty thang. Lived plumb t'other side of the mountain. See, the pains hit her early, and she clumb plumb up to Maw's 'cause her man weren't home to come fetch her. He's off on a loggin' run. He wus good to Janie. She wus mighty purty, and he bought her nice dress-up thangs when he could—hats and gloves and thangs. He never got over it when she died. I like to never, neither.

After my first grief I got all riled up with God hisself. I stomped my feet and hollered at 'im. Well, I hollered at Maw, but I knowed He's listenin'. "What kind of God you got anyway? Fer years you been traipsing all over the country helpin' other folks. Is this yer reward *(pronounced "ree-ward")?* Is this what you git? You tellin' me God couldn't do nothin' to stop it? All this stuff you been tellin' me 'bout God didn't hold to it when it come right down to it, did it? Tell you somethin' else: All your grown days you been givin' the Lord the first fruits of ever'thing you got. Well, I guess that warn't enough for Him. I guess He wanted the first of yer grandbabies too! It ain't right! It ain't right."

Maw made me go on back to church, but I never ag'in could sing "Pow'r in the Blood." I watched her die. I was a rebellious house—a rebellious house. Then one day Charlie came around, and I liked his looks, and he wus sweet to me, and I just up and took up with 'im. It shamed my maw. But what did I care what she said anymore anyway? Her and God wus jest like that *(gesture two fingers pressed together),* and I didn't believe in no merciful God no more. I was surprised how easy it was to ignore 'im. I mean, I didn't git struck down with sickness or nothin'. Charlie was good enough fer me, and I worshiped him. He gimme ever'thin' Maw taught me about love offerin's. I give him the first of my day and the first of my night. The first of my energy was spent doin' fer him. When I baked, the first batch of sweets wus his, and when I cooked, the first and biggest helpin' went to him. That spring when he set off to Nashville to better hisself, I wus the first to wish 'im well—and the last to know he wodn't never be com'n back. All them thangs I done for 'im—I reckon it warn't enough. But the fear of birthin' babies wus jest too keen—too keen.

I didn't let on like it bothered me none when Charlie didn't come back. Let me tell you what I done. My paw told me this story afore he died, about gittin' a hand-me-down winter coat. It wus about three sizes too big, but his maw made him wear it to school anyway. Well, the kids made sech fun of it that ever' mornin' he'd hide it in the woods soon as he got out of sight of his house, and walk to school in his shirtsleeves. In the evenin's he'd find it and wear it back in the door at home. That's how I done my love for Charlie. I's thinkin' about it the other day. When I went out in public, I hid my love at home so's nobody would laugh at me. But when I got back, I wrapped it around me like a big old coat, pulled my head down inside the collar, and buried myself in it. Trouble wus, it didn't have no warmth to it no more. I felt 'bout as cold as Paw's coat must've felt to him after it laid in the winter woods all day. Sometimes I'd put on this hat and dance around, pretendin' I wus a fine lady with a handsome beau that thought I was the world in all. Trouble wus, pretend *(pronounced "pree-tend")* only lasts so long. 'Bout the middle of the night a feather bed can git jest as cold as a creek bed, and a pillow jest about as wet. And God . . . God can seem jest as deaf as a creek stone.

I guess you think I'm gonna tell you some big miracle took place and I come to my senses, but that ain't the way it wus. To tell the truth, when winter come, I didn't have much choice but to go back to live with Maw. It ain't like mountain folk to turn a body away, but still, they can be stern when a body gets wronged. I knowed I'd hurt Maw. That's why I hadn't been to see her all that time—and I dreaded going back. I don't know what I expected 'xactly, but it wus anything but what I got. When I crossed that footlog—I can see her yet—she let out a whoop and slapped her thighs like she done, and stood there grinnin' till she was huggin' me as tight as she closed one of her Mason jars. That sealed it too. Long as she lived, she never asked no questions, never laid down no rules, never oncet let me see the wounds I done caused her.

You cannot even conjure how good that first plate of her green beans tasted. Ever'body else had done left the table when I took out my third plateful. I looked up and she wus watchin' me, and she jest whooped and slapped her thighs. I kept waitin' fer the new to wear off and the bitter to start seepin' out. I mean, she'd done lost a lot more than I had. How could she be so blame happy? I watched fer her to pounce on me like a hen on Sunday dinner. How could she jest keep on bein' so full of love, as if nothin' had ever happened? I tell you, it wus more than I could conceive of. It bothered me right smart. Caused me some wonderment too. I mean, if I liked the way she wus, and I did—I admired her to no end—and if livin' with God made her that way, and she wasn't sour on me, how could I be sour on God? I come there ready to stand my ground, but folks, they jest ain't no arguin' with that kind of love. It don't quit givin' somethin' jest because it loses somethin'.

It wus as painful as birthin' any real baby, and it took a spell longer, but finally, gradually, a new spirit wus born out of me—healthy. Like Paul said in the Bible, "First they give their own selves to the Lord." I went back to church, started givin' my firstfruits to God ag'in—the first 10th of anything I got. Now it's a way of life fer me. I learned herb medicine, and even got where I could watch Maw midwife oncet or twicet afore she died. I been right proud of myself. Then the other day I laid in the creek where there's a little drop-off, and it makes a nice spout where we catch our drankin' water—anyway, I's settin' up there ponderin', and it come to me jest as clear: Now ain't you somethin', Sary Mae? You been givin' yer firstfruits all this time, lah-de-day. You been thinkin' 'cause you're a tither you got this givin' thang sewed up neat as a flour sack. Sure, Sary Mae, the first time this creek thaws out after being froze all winter, you might give the first bucketful to a sick neighbor. But what if there wus a drought and the creek was dryin' up, would you be willin' to give yer last bucketful?

So what I got figgered is this: Givin' the first part of somethin' you have to the Lord is one thing, but it come to me that real offerin', a real holy ground offerin', would be to give the last of somethin' you got. This hat is *(takes off hat)* the last thing I own that belonged to my sister Janie. *(Takes off ring)* This ring is all I got left of Charlie, wherever he is. *(Pause)* And this here *(picks up paper bag and removes jar; leaves bag on stage),* this is the last jar of Maw's green beans. I wus savin' it for Christmas dinner. Well, I'd like to stay and hear what you'ns brung, but I gotta git on back. I'll jest leave these here on the altar. *(Hugs items to self and bows head for a moment, then places them on altar. Backs away a few steps, still looking at altar. Whoops, slaps thighs. Turns, grinning, picks up shoes, and starts out. As she goes, she says:)* I feel like I could skip all the way to Nashville! *(Exits)*

Be Still
Practicing Meditation

Reach Out!

Learning to overcome negative thoughts and stay mindful is not the same as fighting depression. Do you feel overwhelmed by sadness? Remember, you matter. You are not alone. If you need help, reach out. Talk to an adult you love and trust. This could be a teacher, school counselor, or family member. Make an appointment with your doctor. Seek professional help. Or call the National Suicide Prevention Lifeline at 1-800-273-8255. Someone is available to talk with you 24 hours a day, every day.

45TH PARALLEL PRESS

Published in the United States of America by Cherry Lake Publishing
Ann Arbor, Michigan
www.cherrylakepublishing.com

Reading Adviser: Marla Conn, MS, Ed., Literacy specialist, Read-Ability, Inc.
Book Designer: Melinda Millward

Photo Credits: © Ollyy/Shutterstock.com, back cover; © Pollyana Ventura/istockphoto.com, cover, 5; © Dream-StockIcons/Shutterstock.com, 6; © MStudioImages/istockphoto.com, 7; © Crepesoles/Shutterstock.com, 8; © byheaven /stock.adobe.com,9; © kuroksta/Shutterstock.com, 10, 18; © g-stockstudio/istockphoto.com, 11; © ALEX S/Shutterstock.com, 12; © davooda/Shutterstock.com, 14; © Antonio Guillem/Shutterstock.com, 15; © Di Studio/Shutterstock.com, 16; © LightField Studios/Shutterstock.com, 17; © PaytonVanGorp/istockphoto.com, 19; © Aaron Amat/Shutterstock.com, 20; © Olkita/Shutterstock.com, 22; © Africa Studio/Shutterstock.com, 23, 24; © bsd/Shutterstock.com, 26; © Luke SW/Shutterstock.com, 27; © Taliadreams/Shutterstock.com, 28; © 4x6/istockphoto.com, 30

Graphic Element Credits: © kkoman/Shutterstock.com, back cover, front cover, multiple interior pages; © str33t cat/Shutterstock.com, front cover, multiple interior pages; © NotionPic/Shutterstock.com, multiple interior pages; © CARACOLLA/Shutterstock.com, multiple interior pages; © VikiVector/Shutterstock.com, multiple interior pages

45th Parallel Press is an imprint of Cherry Lake Publishing.

Library of Congress Cataloging-in-Publication Data has been filed and is available at catalog.loc.gov

Printed in the United States of America
Corporate Graphics